This Ain't A Joke

Reginald "Dunbar" Walton

This Ain't A Joke

Poems by: Reginald "Dunbar" Walton

Front Cover Picture by: Reginald "Dunbar" Walton

Design by: Jazzy Kitty Publishing

Logo Designs by: Andre M. Saunders/Leroy Grayson

Editor: Anelda L. Attaway

© 2012 Reginald Walton 1-761520301

ISBN 978-0-9851453-2-3

Library of Congress Control Number: 2012906647

All rights reserved. This book is protected under the copyright laws of the United States of America. No part of this publication may be reproduced or transmitted in any format or by any means electronic, mechanical, or otherwise, including photocopying, recording or any other storage or retrieval system without written permission of the publisher, except in the case of brief quotations embodied in critical articles or reviews.

For Worldwide Distribution. Printed in the United States of America. Published by Jazzy Kitty Greetings Marketing & Publishing, LLC. Utilizing Microsoft and Adobe Publishing Software. Scripture quotations are taken from the King James Version of the Holy Bible, and from the Holy Quran. Utilizing Adobe and Microsoft Publishing Software.

DEDICATIONS

This book is dedicated to everyone I ever came across in life because ultimately, you are my teachers.

TABLE OF CONTENTS

Introduction	i
Travel with The Pure Sun	01
The Message	05
U3	07
2 to the Sky	09
What'z Up	12
The Morning of September 30TH	14
Street Life	90
The Chameleon Queen	18
Eye Cry	21
I'm Not Like You	24
The Reunion	26
Daddy's Concentration in Colored Camps	28
Solar Science	33
Next Level Shit	35
Yellow Equality	37
Black History	39
The Attack: Hidden Like Stealth	41
Insects in the Wind	44
The Purifier	46
Directions to Decisions	48
About the Author	50

INTRODUCTION

This book is hilarious. This book is sad. This book is genius. This book is everything that you would ever want to see in a book, on the television screen or on the radio because what you are about to read is real life manifested through written words of wisdom for your clear comprehension. This author has truly been there and expresses himself thoroughly in his writings. You will experience the love, pain, joy and disappointment of a Blackman, who was stripped of his childhood as a youth.

"This Ain't A Joke" is an inside look at what's really going on from someone who is "in the know". Mature enough for someone that is 75 to contemplate his or her thoughts on; real enough to move someone who is 20; and yet simple enough to enhance and enlighten the youth. This book is nature in all of its essence. If you're alive, you will enjoy it.

TRAVEL WITH THE PURE SUN

Back in Ancient times
We used to honor the Gods
In the wilderness of North America
The knowledge of God is really Lost

Hidden and suppressed
By those who have power
In a presidential speech
Not once did they mention Allah

By keeping you blind to God
You'll never see the truth
They fill your head up with dumb shit
Through media news

Paris Hilton got caught
Lindsey Lohan's a junkie
My baby mother's in the projects
In need of some money

The Yankee's made the playoffs
Derek Jeter scored twice
But 2 bums on the corner
At night sleeping with mice

Most hear the words that are spoken
But very few will comprehend
It's Friday night
They out drinking
So their brains not working

Hypnotized by the music
The beat of African drums
Is a subconscious reminder
Of where they brought you from

They installed a process
That's a hands off system
So that they won't have to do shit
Like calling you nigga

You see the truth is
Blacks built and ran this country

From the beginning
But we ignorant to English
And couldn't recognize the sinning

From a Caucasian race
But you know when something's wrong
We kept our faith in the will of God
While singing our slave songs

But through the years of deception
Our children lost perception
Of who we really are
And God used like a weapon

It was this movement and that movement
To move the minds of many
We got the biggest brains on the planet
And our head still empty

But the potential is there
For you to create what you want
That's what these crackers not teaching
To make sure that you don't

I'm connected to the presidents
And all the secret governments
Me and my family
You know we running this shit

Plus these devils want me gone
For interrupting their plans
They said I know too much
I'm growing out of their hands

On this Earth
Naturally the wind blows where it may
Manifested Divine Gods
Here to enforce the judgment day

THE MESSAGE

Tyra cry me river below the belt
Here's a message
Your heart's felt

Been with these weak individuals
But I'm sending them to hell
For getting in the way
Of the righteous supreme God

Burning a path of fire
Scolding lives
Permanent scares
They're babies of life
Two physical eyes but they're still blind
I guess they thought I was playing
When I declared that you mine

Some even showed disrespect
When your beautiful face once appeared
Once again drunk off my spirits
An empty bottle to queers

Not just once
Because the 85 are lost
I rather slug 'em in the brain
Than waste my precious time in thought

There's nothing like your own
You held me down for a while
Despite my stubborn ways
I know you seen Green Mile

I'm a little skinny fellow
Biggest nuts on the block
With an illuminating presence
That can shine through the dark

I even rode for your sister
The one that sing
They call her Mary
I guess y'all got something in common
Why do I worry?

U3

To my father "G" od

How are you doing out there in Heaven

I got plans to make this music

So I use this format clever

There's no money in rapping

So I'm not trying to get rich

Just a recreational art

That can elevate my dome with

Being a man is not easy

I see the weak everyday

You a strong motherfucker

You and moms raised me this way

Or at least you did what you could

When you could you did good

You shined on my mom

I received her reflection and understood

But you intake the wrong food
Which make you other than yourself
I learn my lessons from y'all
So I strive for perfect health

I'm not writing to dis you
Or to stir up any mischief
I'm just paying my homage
To a certain individual

Certain things that you did
Or at least, tried to accomplish
But I was living for the day
Because the next wasn't promised

These are sprouts from a tree
That took a fall like a seed
I stand alone in this world
As a man I should be

2 TO THE SKY

Me and the devil

Lately...

Been battling for supremacy

In Armageddon times

I use my mind to conjure remedies

Navigating through a hell

Made of steel and stone

Elevate on illumination

Makes a heavenly dome

You see my third eye see

Everything my brothers won't see

So 9 times out of ten

I'm thinking for these dummies

Dumb because they're not consciously aware

What's in the air

I used to walk the streets at night

Look up and you was there

Just as clear as the sun
Reddish orange in setting mode
And just as quick as you came
You left me out in the cold

But at least I know you're real
What's meant by time stands still?
Been finding the answers to questions
Tell me how does it feel

To be who you are
And still possess the forgotten
The things that people want
But take for granted like knowledge

Technology rapidly excelled
Ever since 1947
Like we got miraculously smart
And yours ain't crash from out the heavens

We are who we are
God cipher divine is original
There were only the righteous ones
Before divine-evils made us criminals

It's like they stole from me
And said my brother committed the evil
We take the head off the creatures
Because their nature's deceitful

I used to think you were gone
But at times I feel your presence
There's nothing spooky about it
Cause I took time to study lessons

And through my observation
I realize the world is mine
I'm just taking it back
Because the devil's out of time

WHAT'Z UP

What'z up WORLD
Peace to the little boyz and girlz
360° stimulating swirlz

Recognize that your thoughts
Formulate before you speak
Slow down to get down
Then you move your cheeks

In other words
Sun, you just got to do the knowledge
I never said nothing 'bout going to college

Keeping peace within self
Let her manifest health
And keep the devil off the part of the earth
Where I dwell

Any violation
Immediate extermination
Probation violation when I was incarcerated

Took time out to build
Strong righteous foundation
There were obstacles in my path
Because of some hating

But I elevate
Beyond the normalcy of society
Hopefully I'll put it to use
And get the hell up out of poverty

Life is a test
And many feel it's a curse
It's all good
I didn't feel like writing this verse

THE MORNING OF SEPTEMBER 30TH

Now me being God

I got to show & prove equality

To everything in life

Like in wisdom if you follow me

Which mean

Equal access to understanding planted

With sparkling jewels

That reflects on all the planets

Don't bring me no jealousy

I shine

So be secure

Because the earth spins

The moon shines

The sun bring the cure

So that things can be seen

And the planet is fully nourished

There's a single source of energy

The solar system cherish

There's positive and negatives
God, devils, and other things
Learn to love 'em all
You start to understand existing

Planets stay separated
Spinning in perfect harmony
Three hundred and sixty degrees of pure astronomy

Through the clouds of deception
I provide a perception
Send illuminating sparks of light
In that direction

Fuck a protection
It's our natural way of life
If you understand what I'm saying
Than I guess you're my wife

STREET LIFE

In the streets for like a month
Without food, clothing and shelter
Winter time
On the bus
Is where I laid my head brah

Catching Zzz's on the train
You know the Maryland transport thang
With 2 changes of clothes
And some books I had to cling

To like children of the matrix
And my lessons from the nation
Original lessons from Elijah Muhammad's creation

I chose to take that path
Just to gather the experience
Stealing from Lexington Market
And robbing the local residence

But for some odd reason
I was a woman's attraction
Communication problems led to unsatisfaction

Women from all over
Even out of state
Collecting address and numbers
But my moves was too late

One day early in the morning
On the light rail
I was sleep
Awaken by the angelic voice of Lisa
That was deep

'Cause we started to kick the bo-bo
And she told me 'bout her job
Asked me if I wanted one
No longer have to rob

THE CHAMELEON QUEEN

Back in 2000
I knew a light skin Shorty
Resided in west Baltimore
Another chapter in the story

Reaping CBS hard
With that bullshit city job
Plus was fighting a body
Connecting fist into jaw

Sometimes I think back
I could've been more supportive
Seven years for the body
Sentence sanction court ordered

Could of, would of, should of
Got you when you was vulnerable
By shaping and molding you
I could've made a perfect globe

Not crying over milk that got spilled
But on the real
If you want somebody in your life
Let me know deal

Whenever I spoke
It's like you was paying attention
Amazed that I was bombing your brain
Like a nuclear invention

Time can change situations
And that's an actual fact
So I won't chase behind your stinky butt
And try to keep track

I got fired from the job
I ended up smackin' Toshika
For a personal reason
But she can get it where she leak at

"THE RESURRECTION"

I swear I think some witches
Is calling out to the essence
Asking the righteous ones
If they can assist with my presence

By summoning to earth
Collecting correctly elements
An organized occult
Probably targeted for sin

But they want to see a change
What change?
It's unknown
I guess they fed up with the ways of the world
And it's shown

So here I appeared
Without a conscious thought in head
A memory lost
I been sleep for some years

So I journey through the land
Slowly regaining my power
Recalling my memory
A descendant of Allah

Surrounded by angels
To the human eye
Invisible
Silence is a must
I learned my number one principle

The devil's been ruling now
For so many years
So they send me on a mission
Destroy evil in the heads

Of the masses of people
And this here's how I documented
Cemented in time
And every single word
I meant it

EYE CRY

If the God was here today
I'd hold gunz with Bob Marley
Screaming more fire at the top of my lungz
On stolen Harley's

Because the world is corrupt
The rich not giving a fuck
About the masses, cause they ignorant
But I never give up

With a murderous plot
To destroy the weak and wicked
Those with no souls and bitch made
I single out my enemies

My weapon of choice
Is silent without voice
And my style is methodic
Genocidal when I'm on course

Because there's heroes and villains
But I'm considered a felon
Some type of outlawish fugitive
With a divine evil weapon

While societies that's secret
Keep on holding those meetings
If the public really knew
They'll get destroyed by those people

But since they haven't got a clue
The people are easy to mislead
I'm awoke to their wicked wayz
I make the cowards bleed

It's like the venom of a snake
I internally penetrate
If you choose to be my opposition
I put it in your face

I'M NOT LIKE YOU

I started poetry

As a way to channel violence

Silence wasn't really working

Had low patience and tolerance

At first, my lyrics was there

But I just couldn't catch a beat

Street disciple to many

Continue writing in the sheets

But now I mastered the art

And haters hide up in the dark

Thoughts dark for a coward

Hiding, ducking behind the law

Psychological chains

Mostly physical thangs

Drain the strength of a soldier such as self

But I remain

I try to be lyrical

But these pussies keep on pushing me

Jealousy is detected
Plus the evil known as envy

Any intruders with no intelligence
Irrelevant
I let it be known
That my flow's forever celibate

THE REUNION

Patricia, how you doing?
I know it's been a long time
I got your info a few months ago
Now I'm writing this rhyme

Because you used to be a friend of mine
And often silent
With the wisdom of a gray sphere
Reflecting rays of ultra violet

The sun and the moon
But not complete without stars
Like man, woman, and child
This universe can be ours

I been locked for a few years
I know some things might've changed
I got caught up in some drama
The situation strange

I could've handled things different
But I don't regret my decision

Nobody was killed
Good health and still living

Spend time reading
Studying my lessons
The wisdom of ancient sages says that:
Everything's a blessing

I wrote a couple of books
And some albums for entertainment
Used my mind productively
To collect my future rent payment

Until I get a mortgage
Plans in memory storage
But back to you -N-I
I know that issue was boring

I need a strong woman on my side
A real lady in public
That I can share my deepest thoughts with
Without all the rubbish
Someone that's going to trust me
In intimate conversations

Without any jealousy
I can do without the hating

Someone who truly like me
And maybe can learn to love me
Except me for who I am
And vice versa to she

Do you remember the time
I got your number on the bus
I called you a couple of times
Only answering services received my trust

But it's all good
That's the reason I'm writing you now
Like Erykah Badu's lifetime
It's been awhile

DADDY'S CONCENTRATION IN COLORED CAMPS

Shackled to Yakub

The grafted type of person

Why does Muhammad-Muslims murder the devil

Without rehearing

From 35 to 50 years

We make him study hard

The purer his refinement

Delayed slaying by the God

Call 'em by their Father's name

I read in the Holy Qur'an

Elevate on understanding

Attitudes will be gone

Been studying Buddhism for peace

It's in my 120 sheets

Analyzing every lesson

Break it down like its meat

Even though I'm strictly vegan

I only eat from the earth

Equivalent to the presidents
Let's get free, that came first

But don't get hooked on the lyric
Just remember when you hear it
And Bizzy Bone's-Heaven'z Movie
Singing my spirit

But other than that
Just use your lessons as your eyes
Don't ask about my family
I'm all alone and they died

I study knowledge wisdom cipher
Researching the mother plane
Discovery existences
To 85, I seem strange

I'm trying to eat right
Health-wise is my focus factor
The mother plane, of course
Elijah's message to me is data

Iron shirt and tai chi
Is what I perform in the yard
But the essence of it all
Is a calling from God

I don't expect visitation
But for powers, I'll make exceptions
It's the path of a warrior
Through clear Asiatic perceptions

I have to put you on the list
So please, write back to this
Natural rhythm of life
That'll get you high like cannabis

Am I good for a money order
I could use a television
They got X boxes and Playstations
You can order in this prison

Prison?
Not with mind over matter 'cause I be gladder
Than most people on the inside and out
That love to chitter chatter

Misery loves company
But not the individual
Like if I get the flu, you got the flu
I'm not ya average criminal

For so many years
Such a compassionate heart
No one to receive
My shit keep spreading apart

But I mend it together
I keep some needle and thread
That's the way it belongs
Like the earth and its Atmospheres

SOLAR SCIENCE

You have to forgive me
I'm not used to getting responses
So I'm a little more excited than usual
In correspondence

Do you realize
That this is the first time I seen you
In 7½ years
We strangers as people

That separated me
Locked down inside these dungeons
You went whatever way that you went
Like distant cousins

But never the least
I'll leave that shit in the past
So here's my information
So I can see your pretty ass

Mondays and Fridays
9:00 am - 3:00 pm

On Saturdays and Sundays
You can see me again

At the same times
But the days have to be odd
Like 1-3-5-7
Come with an open heart

I've been learning a lot
As far as self-education
And right now
Parapsychology is what I study while waiting

To be released from this bondage
And manifest all my plans
Oh yeah, Neka going to be Neka
We still going to be fam

NEXT LEVEL SHIT

Most girls dress with a sexy look
No extra room for packing
So they carry a pocket book

Exciting crooks and getting tool
Tortured and raped
If you didn't want that attention
Why the hell you dress that way

If you going to show off your body
Go hard and walk as nude
With your ass and titties jiggling
For the rest of these dudes

People travel in crews
That's how it is in America
Hookers and hoes are no different
From the "average" girl in the area

In the NFL
They wear helmets and shoulders pads

Professional Fuckers
Advertise titties and ass

If you a woman of respect
You should wear a long dress
Leave that broken hearted playing field
For the rest to manifest

Sometimes you'll be lonely
Because America is filled with ignorance
There will be guys that you want
But they're filthy with no intelligence

That's when you pull down your panties
In the presence of none
Put your fingers on your clitoris
And spazz out hun

I'm on some next level shit

YELLOW EQUALITY

Miss Kim with the two children

Oriental dealing

Feeling that it's a must

That I express with you my building

On a passionate issue

From this semi-criminal

Outlandish to the law

But I'm righteous like pencils

I'm writing you to let you know

That I really dig your picture

With you laying on the bed

Make me sinful like scripture

Plus the other one you printed out

You posted by the window

With a photographic memory

Make my dick do a demo

Yes it really was sensual

Sexual maybe even

To sum it up in short
You completed my evening

Tuck my dick in my pants
And wiped away the extra cum
Then I had to take a piss
But I'm thinking of fun

That we could have in this world
Maybe chilling together
But any compassion in this place
The warmest weather

Not too hot
And baby not too cold
If you didn't have a man
It's your heart that must be stole

BLACK HISTORY

I decide to perform
In a Black History Program
There'll be hip-hop and poetry
Spoken ways read from hands

Plus they have a choir
Coming in for Black History
Singing praises and hymns
From a white man's religion

They'll be brothers that's negative
Planning to kill the next night
But they'll only kill their brother
While their oppressor watch the fight

I wrote a new song
I'm trying to master for the occasion
Oh, did I mention
This show is sponsored by Caucasians

So they told a nigger to tell me
"We" don't want to hear "nigger"

I'm about to approach me a nigger
Make him see the bigger picture

It's not like I'm using it
In a derogatory statement
I'm just giving the run down
To remind fake haters

After all, it's about Black History
Which is a thing of the past
But that's the same thing that shape the future
Like an hour glass

Knowledge, Wisdom, and understanding
Is the only thing that solve our problems
Can't look yourself in the mirror
So what the fuck you looking at me for

THE ATTACK: HIDDEN LIKE STEALTH

I hide like stealth
I hide like stealth because I am the truth
So who is original man?
According to my knowledge

If God said:
"Let us make man in our image,
According to our likeness"
Then the original man truly is
The maker, the owner, cream of the planet Earth
Father of civilization; God of the universe

Father of civilization
The Father of civilization

Well the Holy Qur'an says:
"Call them by the names of their Fathers
That is juster in the sight of Allah
But if ye know not their fathers name
Call them your brothers in faith"

Well, that said a lot in Surah 33:5 of the Holy Qur'an
Holy because it's pure-un tampered with
Not noble because some ass kisser can highly praise it

I remember reading:
Ye are all gods-sons of the most high
But you will die like mere men
Yeah, they said that
They said that in Psalms 82:6

But way back before then
In the creation of it all
God said: "Let us make man in our image"
So now I'm thinking
Who is they
If God-Allah is one and has no partners

And why does the Holy Qur'an say:
"We created them out of a sticky clay"
It's right there in 37:11
"We" did this, "we" did that
We, We, We, all through the 37th Surah
But Allah has no partners
That's what the Muslims say

That's bullshit
So I'm showing and proving
With Proper Education Always Correcting Errors

I have two eyes even though I'm almost blind
I have to use gravity to bend light to adjust my eyesight
Now I see like you
But I've always heard extraordinary things

I heard extraordinary things like God will make his home
And live with his people
What is the meaning of live

Revelation 21:3 is near the end of the Bible
And I'm near the end of this poem
But before I go
What is the meaning of Revelation?

I hide like stealth
I hide like stealth because I am the truth

INSECTS IN THE WIND

As soon as I come through the door
I hear those crackers talking shit
This Uncle Tom house nigger I'm living with
Let 'em in

He don't like rap
Nor my cultural business
What makes him think I want to hear
Some undercover porky pig hillbillies

I don't...
Never have nor will I ever really want to
A million things occupying my brain
I need some quanjah

To relieve the stress from the days
That come in so many ways
Plus it relaxes me and settles my nerves
The perfect way

Kill a couple of brain cells
I aim at those that remember

In November when the blunt comes around
Its Thanksgiving

There's nothing like the herbal remedy
Of this misdemeanor
That hasn't been blessing my lungs for so long
With its demeanor

I mean I once loved the part of the planet
Called Mary Jane
But from my personal funds and me stacking
It ain't the same

Hip hop has changed
Because the world ain't the same
So if I didn't make alterations
I would be considered insane

THE PURIFIER

Losing my brain

Because my head is on fire

Burning with anger

The death penalty is ignited

You don't understand how I feel

Because you not in my shoes

I gave it to many

And watched their insides ooze

Overflow to the surface

Exposed what they kept hidden

What's really in their hearts

Like a monk on a truthful mission

I took a step back

And watched everything that was in front of me

I'll let the hands of time unfold its fate

Until they come for me

DIRECTIONS TO DECISIONS

I got people that keep on saying they love me
But they don't know me
So in the back of my mind
I got it rooted that they're phony

How can they judge me
They never met me in public
They don't even know the habits
Of what I'm feeding my stomach

I choose to live above it
Put it in the back of my mind
But every now and so often
It takes surface to shine

The smiling faces on the news here
Is very deceitful
You got paid to do a job
That's not informing people

Why do you smile in my face
Pretentious ones in the business

I'll hate to make an enemy
But there was never a friendship to finish

So when it's all said and done
You really have no opinion
Who the hell are you to speak into my life
As if you're dominion

Oh, did I mention
The people that's always wrong and never right and never write
They quick to make a decision
I'm quick to tell them goodnight

And that's just how it is
Every day in this thing we call life
That's why I'm contemplating ending this shit
Right here tonight

ABOUT THE AUTHOR

Reginald Walton was born in Portsmith, Virginia and immediately moved to Baltimore where he grew up at. He spent his childhood traveling up and down the East Coast and never stayed in one neighborhood for more than one year at a time.

By the age of 9, he gravitated toward a life of crime. At the age of 15, he was charged as an adult for an attempt to murder there he was - a child incarcerated with a bunch of grown men that society considered the worst of the worst, but they saw the potential in him and began to teach him. He would listen attentively and decided to make a change. The rest is in his writings. I hope you enjoy.

www.ingramcontent.com/pod-product-compliance
Lightning Source LLC
Chambersburg PA
CBHW071844290426
44109CB00017B/1919